MW00438376

LESSONS FROM
MY MIRROR

Change begins with me

Paula Fuller Enloe

TABLE OF CONTENTS

INTRODUCTION

"The definition of insanity is doing the same thing over and over again but expecting different results." - Albert Einstein

W hen I began to look back on my life, I noticed I had been making the same mistakes over and over, each time, thinking I had learned my lesson. It was at this point in my life, soon after my 50th birthday, that I realized life does not get better by chance, it gets better by change. And the only thing I can change is me.

The first step in my journey was learning to be true to myself and to take ownership of my own choices. I realized that I had been judging myself by what I was intending to do, yet judging others by their actions. That was about to change. I can read the Bible every day and a hundred books on wisdom, but without application, their lessons are only words on a page.

It started with one Post-It® note on my bathroom mirror, followed by another.

On each note was written an inspirational quote or words of wisdom that would help inspire me to be the person I should be. They were there as a reminder every morning to:

1. *Let go of yesterday.*

2. *Keep my eyes off everyone else.*

3. *Focus on changing me.*

No. 1

MISTAKES

For though the righteous fall seven times, they rise again. - Proverbs 24:16 (NIV)

I never meant for anyone to read the notes on my mirror. It was a private war I had waged against myself. Each note became ammunition to help me overcome something I was struggling with in my own character.

One day, not long after I started on this journey of change, my twelve-year old niece and I were on the way to church. We were just having some small talk when the tone of her voice became serious. Our conversation took a turn when she asked, "Aunt Paula, what do you do when you have done something wrong and have asked forgiveness, but the memory of it keeps coming to your mind?"

At first, I was taken aback by her question because I thought, 'She was only just becoming a teenager and yet is already experiencing such deep regret and guilt.'

It was at that moment I became angry at the devil because he knows the young ones are the easiest target to devour, and they don't have a fighting chance alone. So, like a mama bear protecting her little bear cub, I was going to take this opportunity to equip this little cub to fight back.

I began to share with my niece something I had started doing that was helping me overcome some things in my own life. I explained that I was posting notes on my bathroom mirror with quotes to help me become a better person, and putting each note into my daily actions, not just reading them. When whatever I was struggling with would come to my mind, I would think about that note and do what it said. Some were about having a good attitude, not gossiping, or how to grow and be a more successful person.

Every day, I was writing a helpful quote or a word of wisdom about something I needed to work on. I never took one off my mirror, I just added more because I did not want to forget what I had learned. In fact, I worked them into my morning routine by reading them daily before I left for work.

I began paying more attention to and becoming more aware of what I was thinking. If I caught myself thinking negatively or being too judgmental of myself or others, then I quickly replaced those thoughts with the words from one of the notes on my mirror. I was beginning to find that the more I worked on me, the less I thought about how I used to be. This allowed me to focus more on becoming the absolute best version of myself. The more glimpses I saw of my better version, the more I liked her.

I explained to her that one of the most important things we need to learn is how to guard and renew our minds because our greatest battle is in our minds. I then shared these 3 lessons that I had learned in fighting my own battles:

1. Everyone makes mistakes.

The difference between feeling convicted for something we did wrong and condemnation is, through conviction, we say, "I did a terrible thing." Whereas, condemnation brings shame and says, "I am a terrible person." God will convict you in order to change you, but he will never accuse you in order to shame you. God wants you to learn from your mistakes but not punish yourself with them.

2. Whatever happened is done.

We wish we would have done things differently, but we can't change the past. Some mistakes can't be avoided because we just didn't know any better. We were in a learning process. However, there may be times when we get into a situation that we couldn't even imagine allowing ourselves to get into in the first place. But for whatever reason - ignorance, selfishness, or just a bad choice, we did. We have to look at our mistakes as lessons. These lessons, if we allow them to, help us make wiser choices to become a better person.

3. Get back up.

Don't be a prisoner of your past. Instead, use it as a building block for your present. Own up to your mistakes. We all make them. Don't dwell on what you did, or should have done, or should not have done. It happened. It is over. It is what it is. First, repent and make it right, if you can. Then, forgive yourself, which means not bringing it up again in your head.

Although we wish many times we could go back and change things, some of the choices we make do have consequences. What the devil would like to use to destroy us, God will turn it for our good. It may be a lesson learned to make us wiser. He may use it to remove some toxic people in our life in order to bring better people and lead us to a different path. What the devil hates the most is when we use the experience to help someone else.

The healing of your mistakes will not remove your ability to remember them, but it will give you the ability to replay the past without the pain. Sometimes the thoughts of what happened after you've let yourself down just start pouring in and you mentally replay every detail. I explained to my niece how one day, a mistake I had made was tormenting me to the point that I had to physically take my hand and do the motion of pulling the thoughts out of my head and throwing them away. When it tried to come back, I just mentally threw it away again. We must do whatever it takes to tear down those thoughts that try to destroy our peace of mind.

At about that time, I turned my car into the church parking lot and parked. Before opening the car door to exit, my neice leaned over to my side of the car, gave me big hug and said with all sincerity, "Thank you, Aunt Paula!"

I watched as she stepped out of the car and started walking away. I could tell a weight had been lifted from her, even though nothing had changed in her situation. She was in the same body. The mistake wasn't erased away. There may be consequences she could still have to face, but she was different. She was stronger and wiser now. She was letting go of the past and moving forward.

That moment with my niece sparked a desire in me to help others who may be living with regret over something they have done or said. Especially young people who, because of the lies from the enemy, suffer from negative thoughts that they are damaged goods or not good enough because of their past mistakes.

Many mistakes in my life were because I didn't trust my own judgment. I got involved with the wrong people, ignoring what I knew was right and trying to fit in or become like them. I then paid the price to work my way out of the relationship, leaving me back to where I started and to what I already knew was right. But I was on a journey of change. And I knew it had to begin with me.

MIRROR NOTE:

Our greatest lessons
are learned from
our worst mistakes.

No. 2
COURAGE

> *By no means do I count myself an expert in all of this, but I've got my eye on the goal, where God is beckoning us onward—to Jesus. I'm off and running, and I'm not turning back.*
> *- Philippians 3:13-14 (MSG)*

Writing a book about my own mistakes and life lessons has been both challenging and rewarding. It was challenging because I had to become real and transparent. At the same time, it was rewarding because I know that sharing them will empower myself and others.

Knowledge is power, but experience in using the knowledge you gained and applying it, is wisdom. Having the courage to overcome failure becomes a valuable lesson to share with others.

We all have greatness within us. It just takes being brave enough to explore deep inside to find it. I hope this book will inspire and help strengthen others to let go of their past and have the courage to work on the one thing we can all change, ourselves.

Just as I told my niece, no matter what our age, we are all capable of doing things we are ashamed of. In order not to repeat them, we need to try to figure out what caused us to make the mistake, either by the influence of someone else or by our own selfishness. When you see an older person that you feel is wise, it is probably someone who has overcome a lot of mistakes along the way.

Don't let your mistakes paralyze you — accept them, learn from them, and use them to help you grow into a wiser and better person. And then use those lessons to help someone else.

If you have trouble moving forward from a mistake or a bad decision you made, begin with these quotes:

1. *My mistake does not define me.*

2. *I did what I could to fix the situation, even if I am still addressing consequences.*

3. *I am not proud of my mistake.*

4. *I became wiser through the experience.*

5. *I can't control anyone else, but I can control how I will handle similar future situations.*

Post them on your mirror, in your car, on your computer, or any place you will see them to remind you that you are on a journey of change.

There may be times when we are trying to move forward, but we fall back into an old way. The enemy will come back and say, "See, you haven't changed." When that happens, think of it like this: when you are trying to become better, it doesn't mean that you won't mess up again, but it is no longer a part of the new you. You recognize it now, and all you have to do is get back to your new you, your new starting place. You don't have to go all the way back to the beginning. After all, you are farther along in the race than that. Just pick up your baton and stay in the race. You reach the end of the race by continuing to get back up.

We are all human, and we have all failed. Adam and Eve, with no outside influence, except one seed of doubt from the enemy, failed.

We think of learning as something for kids. The truth is, the learning process never ends. There will always be opportunities to grow. We learn more and gain more from our failures than our successes. It is just hard to see at the time. Some of the most interesting people I have ever met, are those who have failed, recovered and improved.

Failure has helped me to look at how I got to this place, and the Post-It® Notes on my mirror help me to get back up and keep moving forward.

MIRROR NOTE:

Failure is not final.
It is the courage to
continue that counts.

No. 3

GRATITUDE

> *Be cheerful no matter what; pray all the time; thank God no matter what happens. This is the way God wants you who belong to Christ Jesus to live.* -1 Thessalonians 5:18 (MSG)

There were many notes on my mirror reminding me of all of the good things to be thankful for in my life. Nothing turns us into selfish, bitter and discontented people more quickly than an ungrateful heart. And nothing will do more to restore contentment and joy than a true spirit of thankfulness.

You may have wondered, if circumstances were different, or if you were born into a different family, would you have been a better student, more confident, or more secure? While it is understandable for some people to feel cheated out of a better life, the truth is, you were born according to God's plan.

It was God who determined the exact time when each one of us would be born, who our parents would be, and where we would live. He does not make mistakes. He is the master planner. His love will conquer the most terrible circumstances in our lives, and His grace can restore all that was lost.

My parents, Lee and Pauline Fuller, had 10 children, James, Percy, Raymond, Roger, John, Vera, Connie, Roy, myself, and Ralph. I never knew our oldest brother, James. He died from pneumonia when he was 3 years old. With a large family, there is usually a big age gap between the siblings. My brother, Percy, was 16 years old by the time our baby brother, Ralph, was born.

My father worked, and my mother stayed home with the children. My father also drank, and we struggled financially. Growing up poor was hard, especially for my older siblings. Being poor and having a big family taught us about what really matters in life and there are some lessons that came out of it that helped me become a better person.

1. I learned to be creative.

We didn't have a lot of store-bought toys when we were kids. We learned how to be creative. I cut pictures of models out of Montgomery Wards and Sears catalogs to make my own paper dolls. I would spend hours raking leaves outside and use them as walls to design my own house.

My youngest brother, Ralph, was my best friend. Some people thought we were twins because of our blonde hair. We did everything together. I would play with cars and line up plastic army men to shoot with rubber bands with him, and he would make mud pies with me. We found a golf ball one day and developed our own golf course by digging holes in the ground and using sticks as our putters.

My sister, Connie and I loved jigsaw puzzles. Sometimes, we would buy them at garage sales. If a piece was missing when we got to the end, we would cut a piece of the cardboard box and color it to make it complete.

2. I learned to be responsible.

By the time I was 10 years old, I knew how to clip coupons and make a grocery list with the best deals from the weekly sale paper. At the grocery store, I could calculate the total, plus tax, of our bill before we got to the checkout lane.

To this day, I still do small cost-saving things, such as washing Ziploc baggies and will sometimes use milk in a recipe the day past its expiration date if it still smells good. But now my kids always check my food before they eat anything out of my refrigerator.

3. I learned to appreciate the little things.

My older brothers remember when our neighbor changed the motor oil in their car, they would take the neighbors old oil and put it in our vehicle. It makes you appreciate being able to buy oil and gas for your car. Washing clothes in a laundromat makes you appreciate having a washer and dryer at home.

In high school, instead of buying a lunch tray, I would buy something cheaper from the snack bar, so I would have enough money to go to the Friday night football game when our team was playing at home. I learned to appreciate being able to attend fun activities and events rather than feel entitled to them.

Our parents never had the funds for a birthday party. And we never felt we needed one. Ralph remembers one of his childhood birthdays when we were playing outside, and he stopped and said, "Hey, it's my birthday!" After we told him happy birthday, we went back to playing. We were just having fun together.

Thanksgiving has always been my favorite holiday. It is the one holiday that has not yet been taken over with commercialism, where you must spend money on gifts and decorations. I really do love that Thanksgiving does not include gift-giving. Eliminating presents takes away the pressure and anxiety of shopping for just the right gift for everyone. Thanksgiving is simply about enjoying great food and being with the people you love.

As a young child, one of my fondest memories was getting up early every Thanksgiving morning, just to sit on the living room floor in front of the television and watch the Macy's Thanksgiving Day Parade.

On Thanksgiving Day in 2012, some 40 years later, I was able, for the first time, to watch the parade in person, when my daughter, Melinda and I, went to New York City for the first time. It was a dream come true and something I will always be thankful for.

4. I learned the value of giving back to help others.

My mother moved into a small apartment after all of her children married. One summer, when the electricity bill was always a little higher from the Texas summer heat, she opened her bill and became very excited. Her bill had been reduced. A program to help low-income, elderly or disabled customers pay their energy bills was helping pay her bill.

After seeing how helpful it was to her, I began donating a little each month to the program when I paid my bill. My mother has since passed away, but I continue to give to this program in order to help some other elderly or disabled person in need of a little extra help.

5. I learned to respect others.

Because of our own struggles, I developed a compassion for people from all walks of life who are fighting their own battles and deserve to be treated with the greatest level of kindness. It taught me to treat everyone with respect no matter their financial status. It taught me to try to see the world through other people's eyes before judging them or their circumstances.

Several years ago, an elderly man ran into Percy, and before leaving, the man said to my brother, "You kids were some of the poorest I have ever seen. But you know, all of you turned out pretty good."

I would agree with the gentleman. We each have our own families and have worked hard to provide and care for them. None of us have a college degree, but in our family, we have a judge, a constable, a former highway patrolman, a retired correctional officer, and others who work in successful businesses, along with some great stay at home moms.

Even though we didn't have much growing up, we learned to be thankful for what we did have.

That kind of outlook will stay with you, no matter how old you are or how much money you make or don't make. There is always something you can be thankful for.

If you ever want to feel rich, just look at all the things you have that money can't buy.

MIRROR NOTE:

Be thankful for what you have. You can always have more, but you could always have less.

No. 4

INFLUENCE

God is not unjust; he will not forget your work and the love you have shown him as you have shown him as you have helped his people and continue to help them. - Hebrews 6:10

There is no real way to measure the impact any one of us can have on another person's life. Sometimes the smallest things can change the course of history for a person and for all of those that person comes in contact.

One of the strongest influences in our lives is our family. Our birth order, the way we were treated by our siblings, the financial circumstances of the family, the place we lived — all of these shaped us at the time when we were most vulnerable.

My mother was a very kind person. Her kindness was not based on what others did. She believed being kind was just how you should be. She did not have many rules for us, but she did not like for us to get in an argument with each other.

I do not remember my mother ever spanking us. She may have thrown a shoe at us when we got into a tussle or argument with one another. Our greatest punishment was the look in her eyes when we knew we had disappointed her. She would not say a word, and that was enough.

My mother lived a lifestyle of character. She chose right, regardless of the consequences. She never tried to scam anyone. She did not lie on the application and forms she had to fill out for her social security benefits. The only thing she ever asked for was a ride. She never owned a car or had a driver's license.

Although my mother had a positive nature, she struggled with feelings of inadequacy as a parent, due to her physical limitations, her lack of education, and her toothless smile. She lost all her teeth due to poor health and her gums were not healthy enough for dentures.

My mother never held a grudge against anyone. My paternal grandmother once shared the story of a time when my parents were living with her. My father had come home drunk and brought another woman home with him. My grandmother ran them both off and my mother continued to live with her mother-in-law. I had heard a few colorful stories about my father from other relatives. When I asked my mother for the validity of these tales, she would only say, "All of that is in the past."

Outside of my family, one of the most influential people in my life when I was growing up, was a woman who befriended our family when I was two years old. I had been admitted to the hospital with pneumonia in Houston, Texas, where we lived at the time. A volunteer at the hospital, Cecilia Angie, became friends with my mother during my stay there. Mrs. Angie's own daughter had recently drowned, and my older sister, Connie, was about the same age as her daughter. The chance meeting created a bond between Mrs. Angie and my family. After we moved to Cleveland, Texas, Mrs. Angie and my mother continued to keep in contact. She and my mother wrote letters to each other almost weekly.

When I was 6 years old, my father died of cancer, leaving my mother a widow with 9 children. Two of my brothers were drafted into the military to serve during the Vietnam War. When my mother had a stroke, partially paralyzing her left side, my oldest brother, Percy, was sent home from the Air Force with an honorable discharge to help at home. My brother, Raymond, had his entire check from the army sent home every month to my mother.

Our friend, Mrs. Angie, knew from my mother's letters what a struggle it was for my mother to raise and provide for her younger children, who were still at home. Mrs. Angie was an excellent seamstress. Every year, she would buy each of us a new pair of shoes and use her skills as a seamstress to sew us new outfits for school. I remember my mother tracing my feet on paper and mailing it to Mrs. Angie so that she would know what size shoe to buy for me.

Every summer, Mrs. Angie would invite my mother's four youngest children, Connie, Roy, Ralph and myself, to stay with her for a week. She took us on trips to the zoo and local museums. We learned how to swim at the YMCA. Those summers created wonderful memories and more importantly, because of one person's generosity and kindness, a whole new world was opened for us.

I continued to keep in touch with Mrs. Angie after my mother passed away. Mrs. Angie lived to be 92 years old. The lessons she taught me continue to live on in my life today.

There have been many others who have greatly impacted my life. I was fortunate to have schoolteachers at an early age who believed in me. It was not long after my father died, that I began first grade. During those first few months, I cried almost every day at school. My teacher and the school secretary knew my situation and instead of being harsh towards me for my outbursts, they were very attentive and compassionate. The security I felt there also taught me respect for authority.

My greatest joy in life has been my children and my grandchildren. If I ever wanted to be a hero to anyone, it would be them. You can impress the world, but your family knows the real you. Most of my decisions in my life have been based on the question, "How will this affect my family?"

A combination of all these people has helped shape the person I am today. Each has had an influence on the decisions I have made and the paths I have taken.

Each one became a human Post-it® note in my life.

The people who influence you the most are those who believe in you the most.

MIRROR NOTE:

Helping one person may not change the world, but it may change the world for that one person.

No. 5
CHOICES

For I know the plans I have for you," declares the
LORD, "plans to prosper you and not to harm you,
plans to give you hope and a future.
- Jeremiah 19:11

My mother never remarried or dated another man after my father died. As a teenager, I still shared the same bed with my mother in our small mobile home. I was extremely naïve about relationships.

I had just turned 17 years old when a friend asked me if I would go on a double date with her boyfriend and his brother, Noble. Noble had graduated two years earlier from the same high school I attended. Being from a small town in east Texas, I knew who Noble was, but I had never spoken to him. I trusted my friend, and Noble was handsome, so of course, I agreed to go with them.

That next weekend, Noble and I had our first date. We connected instantly. After that, we saw each other almost every day. We lived just a few miles from each other.

Noble's family owned horses and cattle. In the evenings, he would pick me up at my house, and I would ride with him to feed cows out in their pasture. On Saturday mornings, I would go with him to the cow auction or round up a cow that had gotten away from the herd.

We did not go on any fancy dates, we just enjoyed being together. The weekend before Valentine's Day, he was leaving to go out of town on a job for a few weeks. He brought me six roses before he left. We seemed to have it all going for us. Then, like most love stories, things took a turn.

That summer, I found out I was pregnant. I was about to enter my senior year of high school. I was an honor student, and I had plans to go to college. My world was crashing down around me. This was not supposed to happen to me.

I knew I would be letting down a lot of people, so I convinced myself that an abortion would be best for everyone. I made an appointment at Planned Parenthood.

I drove to Houston alone to have the procedure, even though I had little driving experience and had never driven in a big city before.

As I got closer to the building, my eyes were so full of tears, thinking about what I was about to do, I almost ran a street light. As I screeched to a stop, the traffic cop standing on the sidewalk shook her finger at me, warning me to slow down. The only response I could muster was a respectful nod. I am sure she thought the tears in my eyes were from almost getting a ticket, but I really just wanted to ask her to please stop me from doing what I was about to do.

When I checked in, as I was filling out the paperwork, I was disappointed that no one tried to talk me out of what was about to happen. In the waiting room, I was struck by the tea party like atmosphere. There were cookies and punch sitting out on a table. I wondered to myself, "Do they not understand the significance of what we are about to do?"

I sat there, stomach churning, knowing in my heart of hearts that this was all so wrong.

While waiting in the lobby, I met another young girl who looked a lot like me. We started talking and learned that we were both in similar situations.

Like me, she was an honor student and had plans to go to college, she did not want to have a baby at such a young age and she was there alone also.

It felt good to talk to someone who understood how I was feeling. I was about to ask for her phone number so that we could keep in touch, when my name was called.

Inside the examining room, the nurse told me to take everything off, put on a gown and lay on the table. When she came back, I was so naïve, I still had my panties on. "I said everything," the nurse barked, when she noticed I was not completely undressed. As I was removing them, she made the snide comment, "How do you think you got this way?"

I was on the table when a machine was brought in. My heart was racing, and I felt sick. At that moment, an announcement came over the speaker calling my name and saying I was needed at the front desk immediately. Thinking the nurse had heard it and would tell me what to do, I said nothing. They announced it again, more urgently. I told the nurse that they were calling my name. She told me to get dressed and go find out what they needed.

When I reached the front desk, I was informed that it had been overlooked that I was not yet 18 years old. As a minor, it was required that I have parental consent in order to have the procedure. I told them that my father was deceased, and I knew my mother would not consent. I was then told they could not proceed with the abortion.

The decision had been taken out of my hands. I was going to have this baby. A tremendous amount of peace came over me.

When I told my family, they were disappointed, but at the same time, there was no question that I had their support. Noble and I were married at a small ceremony in his mother's house. I enrolled in a program that allowed me to finish high school at home.

During my pregnancy, I read all the books I could get my hands on about pregnancy and babies. Finally, the big day arrived. We were looking forward to having a natural birth delivery, but after almost a full day of labor, the decision was made to have a cesarean section. I was put to sleep and when they woke me, I was told that we had a beautiful, healthy, baby girl. We named her Mickie.

Holding my daughter for the first time changed my life forever. I had never felt so much love for another individual before. She was perfect in every way. All my fears and reservations melted away at that moment.

There are times I shudder when I think how close I was to taking my own child's life, merely out of my own selfishness and promiscuity. I cannot imagine what my life would be like today if God had not intervened on that day. There has never been a time since my daughter's birth that she was ever unloved or unwanted.

Forty years later, I can still say she was the beginning of everything good in my life. Her arrival into our lives brought blessings that continue to this day. She is a treasure. How selfish I was to try to deny this world of this precious gift.

Today, my beautiful, caring, and talented daughter is married with two wonderful daughters of her own. Each one is a treasure and a blessing, yet none of them would exist today had I ended her life inside my womb.

There are many women who went through with the abortion and sadly, even years later, deal with grief and the pain of regret. Regret is a powerful weapon in preventing you from forgiving yourself.

If you have ended a pregnancy and struggle with your decision or have made some other life-altering decision in your past, be kind to yourself. Embrace your pain, and then let it go. Turn your experience into something positive to help others.

When Mickie was 2 years old, I wanted to start taking her to church and teach her about God. However, Noble and I were raised in two different denominations. We had to decide which faith we wanted to mold our child's future walk with God.

My mother raised us in the Baptist faith, although our family rarely attended church. She read her Bible every day and enjoyed listening to Oral Roberts on the radio. We always looked forward to watching the Billy Graham crusades when they were broadcasted on television.

Noble's family was Pentecostal and very active in their church. I was fascinated by how much God was in their life even outside of a church service. They talked about their faith and lived a lifestyle of worship and service to God even when they weren't at church. Their lives began to have a tremendous effect on me and created a hunger in me to know God more deeply than I had known Him before.

I began visiting different churches, trying to find one that perhaps Noble and I could agree to attend together. After some searching, I heard about a church that had just voted in a new pastor a few miles from where we lived. One Sunday, I took Mickie with me to visit. I really enjoyed the service and the people at the church, but I was not quite sure if it was the place for me, so I did not go back.

One Saturday, while Noble was working, the pastor and the Sunday school director of the church came to our house. The two of them were out on visitation and wanted to invite us to church the following Sunday. When I recognized these men, I opened the door just slightly because I was wearing a pair of short shorts. They were very kind and seemed to not take any notice of me hiding behind the door.

Years later, I learned they did notice, and we have all laughed many times at how I was hiding from the preacher.

After their visit that day, I began visiting the church sporadically and convinced Noble to come with me to a revival service. Not long after, I was baptized in the name of Jesus and received the gift of the Holy Ghost. Noble was also renewed in the spirit and we both turned our lives over to God.

I was so excited about this new life we were starting, I went to everyone I knew that I had done anything against and repented. I could not change the past, but I wanted those I had offended to know that I had changed. I also forgave others and let go of the hurt I was carrying inside of me.

Two years after turning our lives over to God, Noble and I had another beautiful daughter we named, Melinda. We dedicated our precious girls back to the Lord, making a vow that we would raise them up in the truth of the Word of God.

We have all had choices to make. There may be some decisions that were the wrong choice, that we would rather not admit, the ones we wish we could erase like powder off a chalkboard. But God prefers to transform rather than erase. He doesn't take our experiences or mistakes away from us, because he wants to use those experiences to shape our future. God can take the broken pieces of our lives and make something beautiful out of each one.

MIRROR NOTE:

God can use detours to take you to your destiny.

No. 6

OFFENSES

A brother offended is harder to win than a strong city. - Proverbs 18:19

Noble and I became active members in our church for many years. We were very involved in children's ministry and taught home Bible studies. If there was an event going on at the church, we were almost always a part of it. You would think that with over 3 decades of service in the church, I would have learned how to be a pretty good Christian. However, the process of spiritual growth is never ending. And I have learned that you are never too old to learn.

I have always had a deep care for other people. Working in the court system as a paralegal for over 25 years, has also given me a strong sense of justice. Like the law, I believe there is a right way and a wrong way. However, with God, there is another way, and I have learned that His way is full of grace.

Once, I was in a position at our church where I felt I was treated unfairly. I felt like it was an injustice, and I was devastated.

The decision that was made caused me to lose confidence in myself and some important people in my life that I had trusted. I was hurt and offended.

During this time, I had become too close to an individual and revealed some things about the situation I was not pleased with. I went too far when I shared some personal information that should have been left unsaid.

My mother's most famous saying was, "If you don't have anything nice to say, don't say anything at all." I should have taken her words of wisdom to heart.

This individual chose to share every detail with the ones I had the issue with. I felt betrayed. I would lie awake at night, replaying my mistake over and over. I asked myself questions like, "What was I thinking?" and "How could I have been so irresponsible?" Or I would tell myself, "I should have known better." I remember the warning signs and saw the caution lights, but I plowed on through like a freight train.

I was completely in denial that the problem could be me.

I remember that the blame, the anger, and the frustration were blinding. Every word I spoke and every thought that crossed my mind had one theme: I was the victim. As others became aware of the change that had taken place, they would ask me about what happened. I was more than willing to share my story, and each time, I made myself right.

I was sowing discord among others, while still faithfully attending church. I was like the prodigal son, only I had not left the father's house. I was wallowing in the pig pen of bitterness. I had not lost my wealth, but I had lost my integrity. At the same time, I was like the older brother of the prodigal son, in that I was mad because God was merciful and had raised up someone I knew some dirt on.

Looking back, it reminds me of a story about a man who had a vision of the armies of hell that would come against the church in the last days. He noticed demons were not riding on the backs of horses but were riding on the backs of Christians that had been offended.

Like those offended Christians, instead of releasing pure living waters out of my spirit, I was allowing Satan to use me to release waters tainted with bitterness and offense.

One day, I was discussing the same situation again with someone else, and I felt something cold flow through me. I got scared, and I knew God was warning me. I had already repented; however, after some self-examination, I recognized that I had not forgiven the others in that situation, or I would not still be visiting those areas.

So, I asked God to teach me how to get past all of the hurt. I was still dissatisfied with the situation and how it was being handled, and my actions only made things worse. I went to His Word for the answer. Jesus said in Matthew 5:44, *"But I tell you . . . Pray for anyone who mistreats you."*

That is not the answer I was looking for. The problem was, I did not want to pray for them. I did not want to bless them, but I knew I had to act on His Word, or I would not be forgiven for my wrongs. Therefore, in the beginning, I prayed out of pure obedience.

First, I bartered with God. I told Him, "Ok, well this person has kids, so I will sincerely pray for safety and protection for their children." The next week I heard their family was having financial difficulty. I said to myself and to God, "Ok, I know what it is like to struggle, so I will pray for blessings in their finances." Each morning, while driving to work, I would pray for them. Each week revealed a new need, and each time, I would make myself follow through on praying for that need.

At first, my heart was not in it. They were just words. However, much like physical therapy, we can't stop just because it does not feel good. We have to pray what is true. Each day, I found the more I would pray, the more I felt what I was praying.

Finally, the day came during my routine of praying for all of those things for them, I began to pray for the person, and I actually spoke their names. When I did, something inside me broke, and a river of tears came rushing out of me.

I began praying for God to bless them in every way. I prayed for good health and financial blessings heaped up and running over. I asked God to bless their children and allow them to grow up to be used of God. I prayed for God's protection over their lives. I prayed for anointing on their lives and in their ministry.

Not only did I pray these things would happen for them, but I meant every word with all of my heart.

I repented and told God with a pure heart that I forgive them, and as I began to pray in that heavenly language, peace and joy overflowed in my heart. Keep in mind, this was all happening during my morning drive. I thought I was going to have to pull off the road. It was one of the most freeing moments of my life.

We have all been hurt and will all taste bitterness in this life. However, we have the choice whether or not to drink it. They gave Jesus gall and vinegar, which He tasted but did not drink. Bitterness is the poison you drink, hoping the other person will die, and all the while, you are being eaten up with it on the inside.

You can't get back at anyone by doing evil to them. Being angry and resentful doesn't change the other person. It only changes you. Most of the time, they have moved on and are not even aware you are still bitter.

We have to be careful when a friend or loved one is offended (hurt, angry, or upset by something someone has said or done).

Should you pray for them and encourage them? Absolutely. However, do not take up their offense, meaning do not get involved or take sides.

We may still carry the offense long after the ones involved have resolved their issues. For instance, a friend may come to you about a disagreement with another friend. You see their hurt and you begin to feel the same resentment toward the other person. After a few days, you see the two of them together at a restaurant talking, laughing and posting selfies on social media.

God gave them the grace to handle the offense and overcome it. The very thing that was meant to destroy them may be the very thing that God uses to bless them. But because you were not a part of the offense, you are not given the same grace to bear it, and instead it becomes a root of bitterness within you. Let it go and be thankful God gave them the grace to work it out.

Don't let bitterness and discouragement keep you from doing the right thing. You may have to work through your own disappointment for a while, but it is not the end of the story. It is a part of your testimony.

MIRROR NOTE:

To forgive is to set a prisoner free.
Then I realized the prisoner was me.

No. 7

INTEGRITY

Let no corrupting talk come out of your mouths, but only such as is good for building up, as fits the occasion, that it may give grace to those who hear. - Ephesians 4:19

I ntegrity is the practice of being honest and showing consistent strong moral principles and values.

A man by the name of J. C. Bays once told this story:

"One day when I was about eight years old, I was playing by an open window and I heard Mrs. Brown confide in my mother a serious problem concerning her son.

When Mrs. Brown was gone, my mother, realizing I had heard everything, said to me, 'If Mrs. Brown had left her purse here today, would we give it to someone else?' 'Of course not,' I replied. Then, she continued: 'Mrs. Brown left something far more precious to her than her purse today.

That story is not ours to give to anyone else. It's still hers, even though she left it. So, we should not give it to anyone else. Do you understand?' I did. And I still understand that when someone leaves a bit of confidence or careless gossip with me, it is his—not mine to give to anyone else."

We gossip because it makes us feel important. It makes us feel like we are in the thick of things that are going on. However, after my humbling experience from the damaging effects of gossip, I feel the less I know, the better off I am. It was a lesson I needed to learn, and I have learned well. Even today, I am very cautious in my conversations with friends.

Show integrity by showing that you won't talk about your friends in a way they wouldn't appreciate, especially when they are not there to defend themselves.

When gossip starts, politely interrupt with, "I don't need to know" and go onto another subject. Only God knows the full story from both sides and why those events took place.

Whenever I start to look at what others are doing, I think of this story I heard about a woman who was ready to leave her church because of all the things she noticed that were wrong. However, when she shared her complaints, her pastor used a full glass of water to reveal a valuable lesson about where we choose to place our focus.

"A lady went to her pastor and said 'pastor, I won't be going to your church anymore.'

The pastor responded, 'But why?'

The lady said, 'Ah! I saw a woman gossiping about another member; a man that is a hypocrite; the worship team living wrong; people looking at their phone during service; among so many other things wrong in your church.'

The pastor replied, 'OK. But before you go, do me a favor. Take a full glass of water and walk around the church three times without spilling a drop on the ground. Afterward, leave the church if you desire.'

The lady thought that was too easy! She walked three times around the church as the pastor had asked. When she finished, she told the pastor she was ready to leave.

The pastor said, 'Before you leave, I want to ask you one more question. When you were walking around the church, did you see anyone gossiping?'

The lady replied, 'No.'

'Did you see any hypocrites?'

The lady said, 'No.'

'Anyone looking at their phone?'

'No.'

'You know why?'

'No.'

'You were focused on the glass, to make sure you didn't stumble and spill any water. It's the same with our life. When we keep our eyes on Jesus, we don't have time to see the mistakes of others. We will reach out a helping hand to them and concentrate on our own walk with the Lord.'"

At any church or company, there are going to be things to complain about. People are not perfect. The only one who is perfect is Jesus. If you focus on what you should be doing, He will take care of the rest.

Be a witness, not a judge. Focus on becoming the best version of you and you will not have time to worry about what others are doing.

MIRROR NOTE:

Where I do not have
a responsibility,
I do not need an
opinion.

No. 8

JEALOUSY

Envy is rottenness to the bones.
- Proverbs 14:30

After I had been working for years in our Sunday school department, a family from a large well-known church moved to our area and joined our church. They also became very involved in our children's ministry. They were fine people and one became a very close friend. Our kids were close in age, and we shared a lot of the same ideas and goals.

At first, I enjoyed having the extra help and support that they offered, but then I began to feel threatened. I found fault with everything they tried to implement. I thought, "There was no need to change the way things were. We have been doing it this way for years." In other words, I adopted an, "if it's not broke, don't fix it" mentality.

The truth was, their ideas were fabulous, and I didn't like it. I didn't like the idea of them doing these fabulous things.

They were just trying to make the church better. I did not see God working to show me how I could be better. In my eyes, their creativity shined a spotlight on my inabilities.

Humility is recognizing another person is more talented than me. That person is smarter than me, so I should learn from them. That person is really anointed, so I could use their prayers.

Jealousy asks, what does that person have that I don't have? Or, why does that person have what I don't have?

Instead of admitting my jealousy and insecurity, I became very judgmental. When I lashed out at my friend over some new and brilliant idea she wanted to implement, I realized how low I had sunken.

We don't know we have jealousy until we see the manifestation of it in our actions. We know what fear feels like. We know when we are mad. But jealousy does not have its own emotion.

We need to look at the outward emotions of fear, anger, and resentment in order to reveal jealousy.

I was overcome by shame. My belief that I was a fundamentally good person was shattered. That day, I had come face to face with the person I was on the inside.

No one wants to admit they are jealous. I was so full of pride, that when I saw what I had become, the revelation almost destroyed me. All I wanted to do was hide in a cave.

I felt like it would be easier to say, "I need you to pray for me because I have a problem with drugs or alcohol." People understand those kinds of problems. But to say, "Pray for me. I have a problem with jealousy, envy and backbiting," is difficult to admit.

Jealousy comes from insecurity about ourselves and the belief that we are not good enough. When we are jealous, we have a critical spirit. We become negative about everything, and we are unkind and controlling. When we are jealous, we want to magnify their flaws or failures because of our own insecurities.

Once again, I went to the Word of God for my solution. *"I know what it is to be in need, and I know what it is to have plenty.*

I have learned the secret of being content in any and every situation, whether well fed or hungry, whether living in plenty or in want." Philippians 4:12 (NIV)

When you are content, you don't have to be jealous. God wanted me to be content in everything He has provided for me. He has given me my own unique abilities and my own blessings.

God, in his mercy and grace, mended the relationship with my friend. She has such a strong character and is so full of God's grace that she even came to support me at my first speaking engagement. Today, she is still one of my dearest friends.

Forgiveness is not saying that what was done to us is all right. Forgiveness means that you fill yourself with love and refuse to hold onto the hatred that was caused by another person's behavior.

When we have been deeply hurt or betrayed by a friend, loved one, or even an acquaintance, it can be incredibly difficult to let it go and forgive them. Some acts seem almost unforgivable, but it is possible.

Forgiveness allows us to let go of our anger and resentment, while still letting us learn from our experiences and grow. It offers us peace of mind, freedom from the past, and the courage to change our future.

Forgiveness is one of the most powerful and loving things we can do, and it ultimately brings us peace of mind and the loving energy we deserve in our lives. Often, when we are holding onto resentment toward someone who hurt us, it's about our ego. We want them to suffer as much as we did.

Forgiveness helps everybody involved move on. Not everyone and every situation is meant to be a part of our lives forever. As difficult as it may be to let people go, whether they are a long-time friend, family member or a spouse, when we forgive them, we create a space for them to move onto their next chapter, as well as ourselves.

I truly believe that people don't go around intentionally trying to hurt others, especially those closest to us. People who hurt us are often in a lot of pain themselves, and they're making choices and decisions based on their own wounds.

The notes on my mirror gave me the tools I needed to make improvements in many areas of my life. Starting each day with a new quote or encouraging message in front of me helped me stay focused on my journey instead of someone else's. When I turned my mirror away from others and toward myself, I saw the truth clearly. I was not where I wanted to be because I was not who I needed to be.

Once I stopped comparing myself to others and acknowledged the truth about myself, the damaging effects of envy melted away. I was no longer working against my friends. I accepted responsibility for where I was and how I got there.

I now enjoy promoting the talents of others by sharing their gifts through live feeds and posts on social media. It has become part my own personal ministry.

Try to recognize that every experience in your life, especially the most painful ones, are lessons that reveal to us what we still need to master. You then have the opportunity to become better if you can avoid holding onto the hurt and disappointment.

Some of our spiritual lessons are to learn compassion, self-love, and unconditional love for others. Whether we feel we deserved it or not, somebody gave it to us. And when we receive such a beautiful and selfless gift from somebody else, we are compelled to give it back. This mutual exchange of grace given between people forgiving each other was a beautiful step forward.

MIRROR NOTE:

Jealousy is counting someone else's blessings, instead of your own.

No. 9

PETTINESS

Search me, O God, and know my heart; try me, and know my thoughts; And see if there be any wicked way in me, and lead me in the way everlasting. - Psalm 139: 23-24

One morning, as I looked at all of the notes that had begun to cover my mirror, I asked specifically, "God, what is it that causes me to act in such a negative way?" One word came to my mind, which was, "pettiness." I was actually shocked. Me? Why would God think I was petty? I knew God was always right, so I began to read and study everything I could about the meaning of the word and how it applied to me.

Pettiness is undue concern over trivial matters, especially of small-minded or spiteful nature.

I realized that the word described me perfectly. I was being negative and judgmental about a situation that I had no control over and had become spiteful about little things.

It is easy to have an opinion about how things are done or how they should be done, with no intention of doing anything about it.

My first step in overcoming pettiness was to stop being consumed with things that were not meant for me in the first place. I did not have to be in the know of everything. All I had to do was what God called me to do. I focused more on what I was doing and less on what everyone else was doing, or what I thought they should be doing. I took some time to be by myself to work on me. It was lonely at times, but I knew it would be worth it.

I stopped checking in every day with some of my friends who seemed to bring out the negative side of me. I thought it would be more helpful for me if I did not know what they were doing or who they were with.

We tend to judge people by what they do or who they associate with. I felt the less I knew, the less judgmental I would be. I decided to hide some friends on social media to keep from seeing their comments or activities that might hinder me from moving forward. I found myself doing better each day.

Transition takes time, but if you continue to check yourself as pettiness arises, your patterns will eventually change, and your character will follow.

I remember looking at my clock on the way home one evening and rejoiced because I had gone an entire day without uttering one negative comment. As days turned to weeks and weeks into months, I began to feel much lighter and happier.

It was at this point when I told God, "If you will just let me start all over and allow me to get back into your presence, I will do things your way and trust the perfection of your plan."

My first position, when we became a part of our church was being a teacher for the toddler Sunday school class. During this time of transition, our church needed a toddler teacher, so I told God, "When I came to the church, this was my first assignment, so let me take this class, and I will be the best toddler teacher I can be. I will put my whole heart into it."

I was happy to take the position, and suddenly, I felt that everything had come full circle. I found myself in the perfect will of God.

At first, I thought I would miss being in charge or being involved in everything that went on around me. Instead, teaching those sweet, delightful babies brought new life into me.

No matter how many or how few kids came to my class, I made a full production of the lesson. I read everything I could during the week about the story I was going to be teaching and prepared snacks that went with the story. I made costumes, so they could pretend to be the characters in the lesson.

My entire week was focused on that lesson. I had no time to compare what I was doing to what anyone else was doing. My sole focus was being prepared for the following Sunday.

The kids and the parents alike loved coming to my class to see what lesson we cooked up for that Sunday. I was no longer insecure about what I was called to do.

I learned to let go of criticism, resentments, missed opportunities, and past mistakes. I let go, and I let God handle it. By doing so, I once again found my purpose.

MIRROR NOTE:

When God has shaken an area in your life, don't try to rebuild it yourself.

No. 10

CHANGE

> *Do not conformed to this world, but be transformed by the renewal of your mind, that by testing you may discern what is the will of God, what is good and acceptable and perfect.*
> *- Romans 12:2*

During this time, there were more changes that were being made at our church. As humans, we love to be in control and so a time of transition can be very painful.

Most people do not like change. In fact, the older we get the more resistant we are to change. Change is hard, but in life, the only thing that is for certain is change.

A baby cries when he is being weaned. It is not that the mother no longer loves her child or has forsaken him. It is a time of transition so the child can mature and walk into his purpose.

When an Eagle begins to prepare her nest, she lays leaves and twigs to where they are soft and comfortable for the newborn babies. But when it is time to teach them how to fly, she begins to arrange the twigs where they poke the little eaglets so they will not want to stay in the nest. It is no longer comfortable.

Like an eaglet, I was going through a time of transition, and it was a very uncomfortable place to be. When God stirred up the nest I had created, and I was pushed out of my place of comfort and control, I felt like a bird falling with nothing to hold on to. I felt alone and isolated.

We are so afraid of change that we don't allow ourselves to let go of things soon enough. Fear of change can cause us to hold on to people and things that are toxic to us out of uncertainty over the possibility of being alone or upsetting others.

I was struggling with all of the changes until I came across a 100-page book, Who Moved My Cheese by Spencer Johnson. It is a parable of four characters who were so used to having their cheese just the way it was for so long, that when the cheese was gone, they each had a different reaction to the way they handled this dilemma. The cheese represented our jobs, positions, relationships or anything we place value on and expect to always be there.

The way the characters handled the change was very enlightening to how I was handling my situation. One of the characters wrote notes on the wall to help his friend find the new cheese. That is what led me to start posting notes on my wall and mirror, to help me to remember how far I had come. I realized I could not change my past, but I could change my habits, and that changed my future. You may not be able to control what has happened to you, but you can control your actions.

Insecurity is like a disease that can slowly affect your life. It eats away at our self-esteem and self-worth. First, it starts out as a small infection, but if left untreated, it can completely consume your body.

God never designed us to be insecure. He never created us to be somebody else. No one else in this world can offer what you can. Our worth was never meant to be found in the approval of others.

Do not compare your calling to someone else. I cannot do everything, but I can do something. Don't let what you can't do hinder you from what you can do.

It doesn't take making big changes to change your life. Small changes eventually add up to a changed lifestyle. Change your thoughts, change your life.

MIRROR NOTE:

All you can change is yourself.
And sometimes that changes everything.

No. 11
PURPOSE

You saw me before I was born. Every day of my life was recorded in your book. - Psalm 139:16

One of the greatest changes my sticky notes helped me with was to overcome being a people pleaser. Because of my past mistakes, I had also developed a need for approval from others.

I began to realize that the reason I tried so hard to please people was to benefit me rather than them. If I could please them, then I felt good. It wasn't so much about how they felt, it was me that I was concerned about. Sometimes, people pleasing can be more about selfish motivations than sacrifice.

People pleasers feel bad when their actions do not please others. They assume responsibility for other people's emotional reactions. I thought if someone was angry, unhappy or disappointed, I could not feel good again until I thought I had done whatever needed to be done to make that person happy again, and if possible, stay that way. My extreme need for people to not be hurt or upset with me, or even think badly of me, was really all about me.

Like I mentioned before, I have always been the kind of person that holds onto things too long. Even when I knew it no longer felt right, I could not let go. Part of the reason may have been that letting go felt like losing, and of course, no one wants to be a loser.

I learned that some things, no matter how badly I want them, aren't meant for me. When we no longer cling to people or positions not meant for us, then sometimes losing can actually be a victory.

One of the first things I had to do to make this change was to remove negative people from my life. I had to set boundaries. This was very difficult for me. I sincerely love people, but I had to say no to them being in my life. Letting the wrong kind of people into your life can be incredibly draining.

Toxic relationships aren't just the romantic kind. Sometimes, friendships with the wrong people can become just as damaging.

Don't spend time with negative people. They try to steal your hope because they have lost theirs. You spend enough time being your own worst enemy. You don't need anyone else to help you with that. It is also tempting to surround yourself with people pleasers who go along with everything you say and make you feel better about yourself, but they are not being real either.

People come into your life for a reason, a season, or a lifetime. We get into trouble when we try to create a lifetime relationship with people only meant to be in our life for a season. They come at a time when you are needing a change or going through a difficult time. These people bring you peace and make you laugh. It was the right time, but only for a season.

Don't be afraid to let a relationship die that was not meant to be. When wrong people leave your life, good things start happening. A seed must die before it can produce. It could be the very seed that is needed so that dramatic improvement can come into your life.

To grow and change in a positive way, you need to learn to truly respect yourself and not worry about what other people think. It is not an easy process, if you are a people pleaser by nature. You have to work at it every day.

I had to reprogram my actions when I saw myself slipping back into people pleasing habits. Be aware of what you are doing because if you aren't, like the quote at the beginning of the book said, you will keep doing the same thing over and over again. You give the power to people to make your life good or bad. In the end, it all comes down to what you allow.

God wrote a book about each of us before we were born. It is like inside each of us is a magnet that pulls us toward our purpose. Each one of us is created to have an impact on someone else.

If you live your life depending on other people's approval, you will never feel free and truly happy. It is like when a prisoner breaks out of jail. He is constantly looking behind him to see if anyone recognizes him. However, if he serves his sentence, the warden will sign papers that say he is free, and he doesn't have to look back. He is free indeed. It is when we learn to appreciate who we are that we are completely free.

Don't let people walk all over you. Sometimes when you're too nice and always giving, you might not know if you are being taken advantage of or being used. Learn how to say no. Your true friendships will be revealed. When you give because you can't say no, it will deplete you.

You can still be the kind person you are and yet stand up for yourself. Live life, smile, and do what is right for you and what you are called to do.

Be kind to someone who is having a hard day. Just a smile or short conversation can completely change the course of someone's day. The possibilities for making a positive impact are endless.

I once read a story about a man who was a rich philanthropist who unexpectedly became ill. Christ appeared to him in a dream to show him scenes from his life.

While reviewing each scene, Christ revealed the value he placed on each of the man's actions. Surprisingly, it was not because the man had given away large sums of money that pleased the Lord, but rather, it was one day when the man noticed that his sister was heartbroken. In an effort to comfort her, he embraced her tight for a long period of time. In Christ's book, this was the man's greatest accomplishment.

There is a great cashier who works at our local Walmart. I always try to be in her checkout line. She has tattoos and piercings all over her, and she doesn't usually have a lot to say, but she is the fastest and most efficient cashier they have. I know she will get me in and out quickly even if the other lines are shorter.

She has no idea that somewhere, someone has included her in a book. But just because she is doing her best at something she is good at, she made a lasting impression on me.

I have a great appreciation for those who live difficult lives yet still treat others with compassion and kindness.

Too many of us believe we have no power to make a difference. You don't have to end world hunger. Just be kind to someone. In a time when people are living difficult lives, kindness goes a long way.

There have been times when I have had my drink bought for me in the car line at Sonic. A smile instantly came on my face when I was told my drink had already been paid for. At that moment, I felt like someone cared.

My mother was in a nursing home for several years. On my visits, she would proudly show off a little magnet or flower that some children came by and gave to her. It was the highlight of her day. Her smile brightened my day as well.

My mother-in-law can make some of the most delicious pies I have ever tasted. If she hears of anyone who is sick or a family member has passed away, she makes a pie for them. She claims it is no trouble at all. Those who are a recipient of her pies are not only receiving the pie, but they also receive the love and prayer she put into it as well. That is what makes them so special.

If you are good at organizing, be the best file clerk you can be. If you are a good cook, cook delicious and nutritious meals for your family. If you work on cars, be the best mechanic in the shop. You don't need anyone to tell you that you are good at what you do.

Make it your goal to be able to lie down at night and say, "Today, I was the best I could be." If you are building your life on Christ with love, what you do will matter for eternity. Keep working on what you are, and you will become what you were designed to be.

MIRROR NOTE:

You had a purpose before anyone had an opinion.

No. 12

BROKENNESS

The sacrifices of God are a broken spirit; a broken and contrite heart, O God, you will not despise.
- Psalm 52:17

I was always afraid of the word "brokenness" because I knew there was pain involved. I thought of being broken as shattered glass that was irreparable. But spiritual brokenness is when we come to the end of ourselves, and we are ready for change.

In order to take me to the next level of where God wanted me to be, He had to lead me to a place of brokenness. I thought I was on top of everything. After all, I had a good position in the church, not to mention I was working at a good job. I had a good family. But I was a free spirit, trying to make things happen my way and for my benefit.

There is a brokenness, like a shattered vase, where even though we glue it together, it is never the same. Something like this may happen to people who have come through the harrowing experience of brainwashing and torture. They can come out "broken individuals" who are never quite the same again.

This is not the kind of "brokenness" God wants. We must come to a spiritual brokenness, where we are at the end of ourselves and ready for a change.

That is the place God had to get me to. I had to learn to yield to his ways and not my own.

It is like when you break a horse. A wild horse out on the open range is no good to a rancher until it has been broken so that he can be used to do the work the rancher needs him to do.

Noble had a horse he raised from birth named, Jack Rabbit. Noble trained Jack Rabbit to the point that he could ride him bareback. He could lead Jack Rabbit by using a piece of hay string around his neck. Jack Rabbit was so in tuned to what Noble was about to do, he could almost sense when Noble wanted him to turn, especially when they were rounding up cows. This magnificent creature even knew when a child was in the saddle and would not move until Noble gave him the command to walk.

Breaking a horse does not mean crushing a horse's spirit but taming his wildness and curbing his will so that all his strength and ability can be harnessed and made useful. Much like horses, if our untamed spirit is not broken and we are not willing to trust God, we can have the tendency to bolt and run in fear or lash out in anger when facing difficult situations.

We do not become weaker by being broken; instead, our strength increases because our strength is properly channeled and harnessed.

God loved me even in my wild, untamed condition, but I could only be of limited use to Him. Once broken, I went from being headstrong, selfish, and unpredictable to being responsible, obedient, and trustworthy.

Another prime example would be an untamed horse versus a war horse. A soldier would never ride a free-spirited horse into battle because he knows at the first sound of a gunshot, the horse would buck, run and throw its rider to the ground. However, a broken and trained war horse is one of the greatest assets for a soldier in battle.

Every growth process involves breaking. The earth must be broken to bring forth life. If the seed does not die there is no plant. The pearl starts as an intruding piece of sand. Just as the universe turns decay into value, God turns our brokenness into our beauty.

MIRROR NOTE:

My real brokenness can be used more than my pretend wholeness.

No. 13
FEAR

There is no fear in love; but perfect love casted out fear; because fear hath torment. He that feared is not made perfect in love. - 1 John 4:18

One area I needed the most training was my faith. I was a constant worrier. My husband was a logger and worked as contract laborer, which meant there was never a steady check. Everything affected his work. If it was too wet, he could not work. Dryness meant the mills would fill up and could not take any logs. I was constantly worried about the "what ifs," and I used that phrase frequently. What if the equipment breaks down? What if we can't pay our house note? What if my husband gets hurt?

Fear kills more dreams than failure ever could. I could not enjoy the good times, for worrying about when the bad times were coming.

Just as I was beginning to stick notes on my mirror and trying to create change in my life, my daughter, Melinda, and I took a road trip to Dallas, Texas.

I had brought a Bible study series called "Undercover," by John Bevere, for us to listen to on the way. If only I had heard it thirty years earlier! I thought I was obedient and submissive, but this message took both of us to a whole new level of understanding in this area.

When it came to household decisions, I always thought I knew best and would not easily concede to another. I could put figures on paper and prove I was right on just how things should be and almost force Noble to agree with me; however, this was not how God wanted me to be. God wants me to trust Him with all authority in my life, from my husband to my pastor to the president. By doing so, I am protected by God. Being under authority is like being under an umbrella of protection. I learned to work with Noble and not against him, believing that God will catch us when we fall, or we would learn how to fly together.

Now, I think of authority in our home in this way:

Jesus is the Chief Executive Officer, with the highest-ranking position. He is responsible for the value, soundness and long-term goals of our home.

My husband is the president, responsible for the regular operations and making sure our work and duties are performed the way the CEO designed them.

I am the manager, responsible for overseeing the creation of an efficiently running household.

It is the same as working at my job. I enjoy the work I do, and I respect my boss. Occasionally, I may offer a different perspective in an area, but how the company is run is his responsibility. I had to come to the realization that how my husband handles the position of president and head of our household, is on him.

That revelation helped me let go of the control I felt I needed to have and the worry that tried to consume me for years. If Noble makes a financial decision that is not wise, and I am praying for him, God will deal with him about it. Furthermore, if his decision causes us some hardship, we will do what we have to do when the time comes.

I struggled for years with being negative and fearful, and I have always imagined the worse. Tension and fright seemed to grip almost every part of my life. I feared we would lose our jobs or that our automobiles would break down. Sometimes, I feared we could lose everything and have to move in with someone, but my worst fears never materialized. There was a time when we did file bankruptcy after we had made some unwise loan decisions and the market went bad. But, we survived, and we learned another lesson about not overextending ourselves.

Even while writing this book, fear tried to rise up within me in the form of crippling thoughts such as, "Who do you think you are?" or "What will people think?"

We are trapped in a private war going on inside of our mind between the positive and the negative. Do not let the lies of the enemy to steal what God has planned for your life. God is working on our behalf, whether or not we can see it unfolding at the moment.

Years ago, our pastor preached a message titled, "Time and a Rose." During his sermon, he handed a young man a rose stem with a rosebud that had not yet unfolded. He asked him to open it without tearing off any petals. The young man proceeded carefully try to unfold the rose. It wasn't long before he realized how impossible this was to do without tearing off the petals.

Noticing the young man's inability to unfold the rosebud without tearing it, our pastor took the rose stem back and explained how only God can unfold the rosebud and in time make it a beautiful flower.

We cannot put our hands-on things that happen in our life and try to rush into what we should be. We must trust God in his timing to unfold those moments, just as He unfolds the rose.

Before a caterpillar becomes a butterfly, it struggles to push its way through the tiny opening of the cocoon. If we were to place our hands on it and try to release the caterpillar out of its cocoon too soon, it would come out with a swollen body and small shriveled wings. The struggle is what pushes the fluid out of its body and into its wings. Without the struggle, it could never fly.

In life, struggling is an important part of any growth experience. It is this fight that causes you to develop the calling within you.

MIRROR NOTE:

> You do not have the luxury of choosing the tool God will use to make you what you ought to be.

No. 14

A NEW JOURNEY

> *See, I am doing a new thing! Now it springs up;*
> *do you not perceive it? I am making a way in the*
> *wilderness and streams in the wasteland.*
> *-Isaiah 43:19*

God had one more lesson for me, and it was a big one. All prior lessons seemed to have been building blocks leading to this one. If I had not gone through and learned from these lessons, I would not have been strong enough for the one that brought the greatest change in my life.

Noble has always been a strong, healthy man who hardly ever went to a doctor. In the middle of August he began having pains in his joints and feeling extremely fatigued. A month later, he began running a high fever and chills one night, so I took him to a small local hospital. After an exam, he was sent home and advised to take an over the counter pain reliever.

The next day while at home alone, Noble heard a voice saying, "Who is the man that can take you from me, and what spirit is greater than me?" It was confirmation to Noble that God was going to take care of him.

Those words impacted him so much, Melinda had a plaque made for her dad with those words inscribed on it. Although, we did not know at the time, how much we all were going to need those words for what was ahead.

After two more days of constant pain, I took him to another hospital in Conroe, Texas. He was so weak I had to push him into the emergency room with a wheelchair. The hospital staff immediately admitted him.

I had already learned by now to trust God to guide our steps, so I knew that God had a plan and He had a purpose. No matter how tough things seemed, I had to trust Him.

Our first blessing upon being admitted was learning that my niece, Vickie, who was a registered nurse, was working at this same hospital and on the same floor. Vickie was able to be with us during the doctors' visits, when they came in each day to discuss his prognosis.

The preliminary diagnosis was that he could possibly have lymphoma, a cancer that starts in the cells of the immune system.

I began to read and study about lymphoma so that I could better understand what was happening in his body.

There are over 500 lymph nodes in our body. Lymph is the fluid that carries white blood cells throughout the body. A node is an intersection where these vessels meet and form a slight swelling knob, like where the leaves stem out on a plant. Lymph nodes work as filters for harmful substances. They contain immune cells that help fight infection by attacking germs that are carried in through the lymph fluid. Swollen lymph nodes tell you that something is not right.

That Friday evening, several friends and family were in Noble's hospital room with us visiting, along with our niece. The doctor came in and leaned over to Vickie and whispered something to her in her ear. Vickie looked at me and said, "You may want to ask everyone to leave for a minute and wait out in the hallway."

It is amazing how in less than 60 seconds you can go from visiting and laughing to alarm and uncertainty. After everyone stepped out into the hallway, his doctor gave us the results. Noble had a more advanced stage of cancer than first thought. He had Stage IV Non-Hodgkins Lymphoma. It was in his bone marrow and small intestine and throughout other lymph nodes in his body. He also had a five-inch mass outside of his stomach.

For the most part, I thought we both took the news well. However, when it was time to tell those waiting, I opened the door and when I saw their faces looking at me with anticipation, I was speechless. I could not say a word. Perhaps it was because there were so many people, or maybe I just could not bring myself to say the words out loud that Noble had cancer. I closed the door and asked Vickie to go out and tell them.

When everyone came back inside, they prayed for Noble and for me. We both felt peace and felt like, at least now, we knew what we were facing.

Our granddaughter, Autumn, who is very close to her grandfather, took the news the worst. She looked at me and whispered, "Does Grandpa have cancer?" I nodded my head, "Yes." She began to cry. I took her down the hallway to a vacant hospital room and explained to her what I knew about what they told us. Then, I told her he would also have to take chemo treatments. Autumn said, "I just want him to come home and shoot the bow and arrow with me again."

Noble spent 10 days in the hospital. During that time, because we had such a big family and many friends coming to visit, they allowed us to move into another room to accommodate them all. We were very blessed to have so much love and support.

We had many unexpected visitors during that hospital stay, including a couple we had given a bible study to in our home years ago. A friend that Noble had not seen in years drove several hours to see him. A young man who grew up in our church came and read aloud Psalm 139, a Bible passage that God had given to him for Noble.

Another minister, who had been previously diagnosed with the same cancer, came to visit. He came to encourage Noble with his testimony and offer his help with any questions we may have along the way.

The kindness toward my family during our time of need was never ending. Our church lived streamed the service one Sunday just so that Noble would be able to enjoy watching it that morning.

One night, after everyone had left, and we were alone in his hospital room, Noble began to weep. He said he never knew he had so many friends.

It was such a sweet, emotional moment, and he described it best when he said, "I feel like George Bailey on, "It's a Wonderful Life." I had to smile to myself about that because that is my favorite movie, and I watch it every year at Christmas time. Noble always hated it.

I think it was because George Bailey never got to be the successful businessman he always wanted to be and that is how Noble saw himself, always facing one set back after another. That night, Noble saw the real meaning of the story come to life.

We all have a purpose in this life. Just as Clarence, the Angel in the movie, wrote inside the book he gave to George Bailey, "Remember, no man is a failure who has friends."

MIRROR NOTE:

Our lessons come from
the journey,
not the destination.

No. 15

BLESSINGS

And we know that for those who love God all things work together for good, for those who are called according to his purpose. - Romans 8:28

Noble was referred to an oncologist who prescribed chemo treatments for one year due to the size of the tumors in his stomach and shoulders. After coming home from the hospital, we spent the first two weeks trying to get insurance for his treatments. My insurance from my job would not cover it. We found out that one treatment could cost over $16,000.

We had a great insurance broker who worked with us every day. He was also a cancer survivor and showed a lot of compassion for our situation. I noticed throughout the many phone calls to the insurance marketplace that the ones who were most helpful had an experience with cancer themselves or in the life of someone close to them.

Compassion moves us into action. It creates a desire to ease the pain of someone else's suffering. When Jesus saw the crowd, the Bible says in Matthew 9:36, *"He was moved with compassion."* Compassion moves us to act. We can have sympathy for someone and offer condolences, but if you have compassion, you feel compelled to help. Our compassion for others has become greater because of our own personal trials.

The day before his first scheduled treatment, we received a call that the insurance we had applied for would cover everything. We serve an on-time God. Sometimes, we go through storms, but if we trust and follow Him, He will get us safely through to the other side.

One of our greatest blessings was our children. They stepped up and took a lot of the work upon themselves. Our daughters, Mickie and Melinda, helped fill out the excessive amount of paperwork that was involved with the insurance company, applying for disability insurance and for financial aid. Mickie's husband, Jake, helped finish the logging jobs Noble had been working on. Our family was always close, but we became closer as we worked together to make all the needed medical and financial decisions.

Noble began his first chemotherapy treatments on October 14, 2016. Not long afterward, Noble began losing a lot of his hair. We would find a large clump of hair in the shower drain each time he showered. It was beginning to fall into his face during the day.

Two weeks after that first treatment, as I was driving into our yard after work, I saw our son-in-law, Jake, walking toward our house with an electric razor in his hand. He lifted the razor up to me, signifying it was time. Noble had decided to have it all shaved off and called Jake. Although Jake wasn't happy about the reason for shaving his father-in-law's hair off, he was honored that he had been asked him to do it for him.

Once again, it was our granddaughter, Autumn, who was most affected by the transformation. She was quite shaken when she first saw him. Although Noble looked very handsome with his new look, to her it was another reminder that her grandfather had cancer.

To lighten the mood, everyone took turns feeling how smooth his head was and commenting on how good he looked with a bald head.

When Noble was still in the hospital, a close friend was visiting and had made a comment that when/if Noble lost his hair, he would shave his own hair. Jake was there and committed to doing the same, although hoping deep down he would never have to follow through with that promise.

Not long after word got out that Noble's head was shaved, Jake received a picture on his cell phone from this friend with his head shaved. A friendly remember to Jake of the pledge he had made.

Jake's first response when he saw the picture was "Oh Snap!" Jake knew it was his turn. But as always, true to his word and without complaint, Jake shaved his head as well.

The biggest surprise came at church the next Sunday. Noble was sitting on the platform when he looked out in the congregation and saw his oldest brother, Danny, sitting on the pew with a shaved head.

Noble began making his way down off the platform and Danny, seeing him, left his pew and met him. Their loving embrace needed no words.

All who witnessed this touching moment were moved to tears. Danny jokingly told Noble, "I left my mustache on so everyone will be able to tell us apart." Danny's son, Joe, also shaved his head in support of his uncle. Danny and Joe are the strong, silent type, but they let the clippers speak the words from their big hearts.

All of these men shaving their heads did not bring a cure for Noble, but it spoke volumes to his heart. They were putting their compassion to work. Their actions said they cared about him and were there to support him through the journey.

I also found that Noble and I had to adjust to his new look. The next morning after he shaved, I was in the kitchen cooking breakfast when Noble walked in. I was startled so much that I jumped at the sight of him. He laughed and said, "That's ok, I scared myself when I first looked in the mirror." He told me how he had begun his routine of getting dressed and when he started to comb his hair, he realized there was none to comb.

The week of Thanksgiving, Jake helped Noble drive to New Mexico to deliver Noble's logging equipment that he had sold because he could no longer work. After three flat tires and 21 hours later, they finally made it. They were on their way back Sunday night, but would not be back in time for our annual Thanksgiving service at church.

During this special service, those in attendance who would like to, took turns giving thanks for their blessings that year. Our church sound system was set up to allow Noble and Jake to talk on their cell phone and still be able to give their Thanksgiving testimony during the service. Tears flowed as we listened to them give thanks for all that our family has gone through and for all of those who have helped us through it.

At Christmas time each year, our church donates food baskets to families in need. Every year our family contributes food or money to help fill the baskets. This year, we were surprised that a basket of food was given to us. I was humbled to tears yet again by the compassion shown to us.

That year, Christmas dinner was at Noble's mother's home with all of his family. The weather was perfect, and we were able to eat outside, which almost never happens. During this time, I noticed how quiet Noble had become. He has always been one to carry on a conversation at length with anyone, and he always enjoyed getting together and visiting with his family on a day like this. This day, however, I noticed he was just sitting and hardly speaking at all. Fatigue is one of the most common side effects of cancer treatment. I knew this was the cause, but it made me sad to see him this way. After almost 40 years of marriage, I had heard most of his stories before, but I found myself looking forward to the day I could hear him tell them all again.

Noble also started having sores in his mouth. When he tried to talk too much, his throat felt like it was closing up, so he spoke in whispers most of the time. He said it felt like a severe case of strep throat. He could hardly swallow.

The taste of his food had changed drastically for him. He could not have ice because his mouth was so sensitive. Anything sweet was magnified to taste extremely sweet. Mustard, pepper or anything spicy set his mouth on fire. He missed being able to enjoy the taste of good food.

I made his favorite blueberry muffins for breakfast one morning, thinking he would enjoy them because they are not sweet like a donut or cake. He took one bite and said all he could taste was the sweetness so strong that he could not finish it.

Undergoing chemotherapy is an unpleasant experience that can radically transform a cancer patient's life. From nausea and hair loss, to fatigue and taste changes, the side effects can be drastic and unexpected. However, Noble's greatest struggle was with what he could no longer do.

During one of those moments of weakness, he cried out to me, "This is like a nightmare. I used to be able to work all day and then come home and work some more." It was hard for him to adjust to his new limits.

That weekend, I took him to the Houston Garden Center and we bought a fruit tree for his upcoming birthday. I felt that enjoying fresh fruit from his own tree would be something for him to look forward to. I wanted to keep him encouraged about our future beyond cancer.

On New Year's Eve, we bought fireworks to celebrate the New Year. I don't normally like spending money on fireworks because to me, it seemed like we were just setting dollar bills on fire and watching them burn. However, this year, I wanted us all to enjoy the moment. We had a lot to celebrate. I was really looking forward to a new year to leave cancer behind and start a new year of good health and more blessings ahead.

January 1, 2017 was Noble's 59th birthday. We started the first day of 2017 by going to church.

Our pastor preached that this year was the Jewish year 5777.

The number 5 in Hebrew means "grace" and the number 7 stands for "perfection/completion."

When it was time to give in the offering, I felt impressed to write a check for $57.77 and put it in the offering, believing and claiming this to be our year of grace and perfection/completion.

After church, our pastor walked up to Noble and gave him a check. He said it was a love offering from the church. The check was for $1,577.70.

Some people wonder why God does not perform miracles anymore. He still does.

Miracles are happening all around us, we just have to look for them.

MIRROR NOTE:

Sometimes God will send us what we need in a package we did not ask for.

No. 16
HEROES

The LORD is good, a stronghold in the day of troubles; he knows those who take refuge in him.– Nahum 1:7

Sunday, January 8th, was our wedding anniversary. Neither of us remembered until we got to church and I read it in the church bulletin. I walked up to the platform before service started and showed it to Noble. We both burst out laughing.

Our kids gave us the most amazing anniversary present. They took us on a cruise to Cozumel. Noble and I had never been on a cruise before. We all experienced some sea sickness when we encountered some rocky waters and high waves. Noble, however, became very sick and vomited for almost an hour. Other than those moments of sickness, the trip was great.

The highlight of our trip was when our future son-in-law, Lee, proposed to our daughter, Melinda, on the ship. It was Friday, January 20, and my 56th birthday.

Lee and Jake spent the day planning the surprise. We were dressed for our evening dinner, and when we walked onto the deck outside, the cruise director called Lee and Melinda's name, announcing they had won a prize. They were told to look at the outside video screen.

On the screen were the words, "Will you marry me?" When Melinda turned back around, Lee was on his knees with a ring in his hand. Of course, she said, "Yes!" We went to dinner and there were roses on the table for Melinda and another vase with a rose for me for my birthday.

Due to a nearby storm, we had to stay on the ship an extra day. I was writing in my journal and I asked Noble to tell me what the best part of the cruise was for him. He replied, "When we get off the boat." He enjoyed being with family, the entertainment on the ship and the beaches were beautiful, but I don't think he will go on another cruise anytime soon. This East-Texas man missed his pine trees.

Noble has always been a true cowboy. He even wears cowboy boots when he is dressed in a suit and tie for church.

One Sunday morning, our assistant pastor asked Noble to come to the office with him.

When Noble walked in, he was handed a box. Inside the box was a new pair of cowboy boots. Noble has never been one to show his emotions, but there is something just so powerful about unexpected acts of kindness that even the least emotional people can't stay untouched by such acts. To this day, when he is dressed in his suit, he is wearing those boots.

One of the side effects of chemotherapy treatment that Noble dreaded the most were hiccups that would last for up to 10 days and nights without ceasing. He could not sleep because they were so severe. No medication or any method we tried could remedy them.

Noble would begin to prepare himself mentally the day after chemo treatment to be ready for the hiccups. It was always sad to hear him hiccup for the first time after his treatment because I knew it would not stop for days. He dreaded them. They were so uncontrollable it was almost maddening.

We tried every remedy we could find on the internet or what was recommended by friends and family. He tried holding his breath while drinking water. Apple cider vinegar and lemons did not help. We even bought "gripe water" used for colic in babies. Nothing worked.

At Noble's next appointment with his oncologist, I asked him to please find something that could prevent the hiccups. I showed him a video of Noble asleep in his recliner, hiccupping all the while he was asleep. The video got his attention and he promised to research it. Unfortunately, he could not find anything more than what we had already tried.

Compassion starts with a willingness to see someone else's pain. Rather than looking away or denying or ignoring their pain, we acknowledge the person's experience and that makes them feel less alone in their suffering.

Not long after that visit Noble was having severe pain in his lower back all night. I called the oncologist's office first thing in the morning and asked if Noble could take some Trazadone because we heard it would help him sleep. The staff said they doubt the doctor would prescribe it because it was not a prescription used in chemo treatments.

I had a feeling this doctor would do anything he could to help because I saw the compassion he had for Noble when he saw the video. Sure enough, about 15 minutes later, the nurse called and said the prescription would be ready for pickup at the pharmacy.

One day, Noble was in Lufkin, Texas where his friend was pouring a slab for their new church building. Noble was having hiccups so badly, he began to have chest spasms. He called our pastor and asked him to pray for him.

A short time later, another minister, who pastors a church in Homer, about 8 miles away, pulled into the parking lot. The minister walked up to Noble and, without even greeting him, he spoke these words, "I am here to lay hands on you and pray them hiccups off of you." Then he laid his hands on Noble and told the hiccups they had to go. The hiccups stopped for the rest of that day.

We heard about another friend who stood in proxy for prayer for Noble at his church in Dallas, Texas one night. Each time the hiccups stopped, even for just a short time, we gave God praise.

One day, Noble's sister, Elaine, called me and asked if we had tried peppermint oil for his hiccups. I was so exhausted from trying all of the suggested remedies, I was almost to the point of saying, "Please don't tell me another remedy." Thankfully, I listened.

She suggested that we put some on the roof of his mouth and on the bottom of his feet. I thanked her and told her I had some peppermint oil, and if they start again, I would try it.

That night, Noble began having hiccups again. I got the peppermint oil as she had suggested and instructed him to put the oil on his finger and hold it to the roof of his mouth.

I put some of the oil in my hands and began to rub it on the on the bottom of his feet. During this time, I began to pray for him as I rubbed his feet with the oil. As I was praying, a dream I had while Noble was still in the hospital came back to me.

I had dreamed that I was with Jesus and attending to his every need. I was washing Jesus' feet, I was making sure his robe was adjusted and brought him food to eat. When I knelt to wash his feet, Jesus asked me, "Why are you doing this for me?" Bewildered, I answered, "Because you are my Lord." Jesus replied, "Your husband is your lord on earth, and he deserves the same honor from you."

At the time, I believed it was confirmation of the revelation I received from John Bevere's "Undercover" Bible study and to remind me that I was under God's protection.

But this night, I began to claim this dream as a promise and as I was rubbing his feet, I began giving him honor as I had done for Jesus in my dream. Noble fell back to sleep and within a few minutes, the hiccups stopped. This time, they did not return.

Another side effect from the chemotherapy was that Noble's feet had become so swollen he could not put on his boots. His face and feet were swollen. His big toes on his left foot turned blue and were painful to touch.

I watched my active, vibrant husband get thinner and weaker every day. He would wake with severe leg cramps in the middle of the night. I would rub them until he could fall asleep again.

There were times when he was sitting on the toilet shivering. I would wrap him in blankets and help him back to bed. It broke my heart to see him in this state.

One night I asked him if he would like a bowl of ice cream. He said he did, but by the time I got the ice cream in the bowl and took it over to his recliner where he was resting, he was already asleep. He wasn't hiccupping, so I didn't wake him. That night, he slept for 10 hours.

During that time, Noble was not able to work at all. But God blessed us in remarkable ways. The attorney I was working for, paid my salary the entire time Noble was in the hospital and allowed me to take off any time to be with Noble during his treatments. My co-worker gave me a get well card with $400.00 cash inside and took on extra files to help me stay caught up with my own work. One of my nieces visited our church one Sunday and handed us a card with $250.00 cash inside.

One church where Noble had preached several times, mailed us a check each month for an entire year, which helped pay for our gas back and forth to the doctor.

We had stopped to eat lunch one day after a chemo treatment at a nearby restaurant and we ran into some old friends. They stopped at our table as they were leaving and inquired how Noble was doing. When we finished our meal and asked for our check, we were told it was paid for. Unknowing to us, our friends had paid for our meal before they left.

There were many others who were so kind and helpful to us during this time, that we will never be able to repay or thank any of these wonderful people enough. None of them gave to us for recognition or praise. It was done out of compassion.

A hero is someone who is generous in spirit and who gives back as much as possible to help people. These people are my heroes. We also continued to be faithful in giving our tithes and offering. God has proven his promise that He will give back to us with an increase if we are faithful in our giving.

One day, we stopped at Tractor Supply to buy a battery for our tractor. Outside the store, there were some rose bushes on sale. Noble told me to pick out a couple of bushes for our yard. I chose a rose called "peace" to represent the peace that God had given us during this storm.

The next evening when I got home from work, our granddaughters and their cousin, who lived nearby, had mowed and cleaned out my flower garden and planted our new rose bushes. The acts of kindness from friends and family, no matter how small they may have thought while doing them, were never considered small to us.

We noticed that Noble's fingernails had become very brittle due to the chemotherapy. I bought some nail strengthening fingernail polish. As I was polishing his nails, Noble said, "Well, I guess I can no longer make fun of Jake, for going to the nail salon when he sees this." Noble had always poked fun at Jake for going to a nail salon for pedicures because he has always thought of spas and salons as women's gathering places. Instead of allowing his father-in-law's playful teasing to hinder him, Jake would respond back to

Noble by saying "I have an appointment with the toe doctor."

Noble called me at work one day and asked me to pick up some cube steaks. He was craving chicken fried steak and mashed potatoes. I was glad to do it because that meant he was feeling better. The meal did not taste as good to Noble as he had hoped because of his taste buds still being messed up.

The next day, I made homemade biscuits and gravy for breakfast. Noble's mother had stopped by to visit and I invited her to stay and eat breakfast with us.

During the meal, I shared with her how Noble's taste buds had changed since he began his chemo treatments. About that time, Noble commented, "I used to not like this gravy, but now that my taste buds are all messed up, it tastes pretty good." We all had a good laugh at how unflattering that sounded.

Cancer taught us that these small moments of happiness are the only moments you can ever really control. You can make them happen every day. As a result, you can make sure every day there is something to look forward to.

Even during the hard times, there was always something we could find that brought us contentment and joy of just being together.

MIRROR NOTE:

Be thankful for the struggle, without it you would not have stumbled across your strength.

No. 17

THE PERFECT STORM

> *Trust in the LORD with all your heart, and do not lean on your own understanding. In all your ways acknowledge him, and he will make straight your paths. - Proverbs 3:5-6*

Sometimes the storms that come into our life help prioritize the things that are truly important. In the Bible, when a storm came while Apostle Paul was on a ship, the crew threw cargo overboard that was not as valuable as the people on the ship. In life, a storm will cause you let go of the cargo of old hurts and past disappointments, in order in to hold on to the things that really matter.

When Noble was in high school, he enjoyed playing on his school's football team. During the game, the coaches would sometimes call time-out. A time-out is a short interruption in a regular period of play called by an official so the players may rest, make substitutions or discuss tactics.

Noble felt like God had used cancer to call him into a time-out.

Even though he was sick and in pain, with eight months of chemotherapy treatments, Noble never went a day without talking to someone about the goodness of God.

He would sit in his chair with an IV in his arm and the chemotherapy drugs pulsing through his veins, telling the next person in the chair beside him of all the blessings God was doing in his life. When that person left, someone on the other side of the room would come and sit beside him to hear his testimony. He felt like this was what God had called him to do in his time-out.

A few months after Noble started his treatments, I received a text from my niece, Vickie, the nurse who worked in the hospital where Noble was first diagnosed with cancer. Her text read, "I know it may be hard to believe, but you guys have helped me so much over the past few months to get some things worked out in my heart."

When I read her text to Noble, he broke down and wept. It was another confirmation to him of why God had him in time-out. He would have never had the chance to get to know her this well otherwise.

We do not have to wait until we are inside the church building to tell others about the goodness of God. *"The smallest portion of my ministry is behind the pulpit"* – Evangelist Noble Enloe.

One night, Mickie and Jake invited us to their house one night to watch the movie, "Hacksaw Ridge," the true story of Desmond Doss, who saved 75 men in World War II without firing a shot. He had a personal conviction that he should never fight or carry a weapon. Enduring ridicule and abuse from his comrades, he stayed true to the end. As he single-handily evacuated wounded soldiers while putting his own life in jeopardy, he prayed after each rescue, "Please, Lord help me get one more."

With what Noble was going through, knowing this was a reenactment of a true story, and the fact that three of my brothers served in the Vietnam War, I could hardly watch the most graphic and violent scenes of the battle.

I could not stop crying during one dramatic scene when the main character was desperately fighting, despite the pain he felt from his own wounds, to reach one more wounded soldier to bring out of the battle and in to safety.

My granddaughters, Summer and Autumn, were sitting beside me, and seeing my tears, asked me, "Grandma, you know it is just a movie, don't you?" Noticing their genuine concern, I did my best to get control of my emotions for their sake.

When you go through pain, you have more empathy for others. You don't want others to go through what you've been through, and you don't wish the pain you experienced upon anyone. It teaches you how to be kind and to never underestimate someone else's pain just because you haven't gone through it yourself.

Cancer taught us to have courage, patience, compassion and humility. Now when we pray for someone, we do so with a better understanding of their pain and suffering.

Six months after Noble was first diagnosed with Lymphoma, we met with his oncologist again. We were told, according to the tests, the lymph nodes and the bone barrow look clean, all under a size 2. We did not realize at the time, that meant there was no sign of cancer.

Even though he was still having pain in his side, but we were told it could be scar tissue, or it may need radiation treatments.

Noble's sister, Elaine, invited us to her house for dinner one night. Noble's mother and two other couples were also invited. We had a delicious meal and visit. Before we left, everyone gathered around Noble and prayed for him for complete healing from the pain he was still having in his side and that he would not need radiation. We could feel the presence of the Lord there when we were praying.

Matthew 18:30 tells us, *"Where two or three are gathered together in My name, I am there in the midst of them."* He was certainly there that night.

When we went to get the results from Noble's final PT scan, our daughter, Melinda, went with us. The oncologist told us that all lymph nodes had reached normal range except one, which is in suspension and looks to be scar tissue. He felt that radiation would cause more harm than good, which was another answer to prayer.

As the doctor was about to leave, Melinda asked him, "My Dad was diagnosed with Stage IV cancer. What stage is he in now?" He smiled and replied, "Remission. Complete remission means that tests, exams and scans show that all signs of cancer are gone." Our prayers had been answered and His answer was "Yes!"

Some doctors also refer to complete remission as "no evidence of disease" (NED). Remission is also another word for forgiveness, the cancellation of a debt, charge, or penalty. The word has so much more meaning to me now than ever before.

It is often through the most difficult journeys that the Lord imparts His most precious lessons. What God allows, He allows for a reason. Nothing comes to us without passing by Him first.

God not only permitted cancer to come into our life, He used it. Instead of cancer destroying us, God used cancer to destroy some things.

Cancer destroyed our pride, selfishness, and other sins we had allowed to become complacent with in our life. It destroyed many of the insecurities I had about myself.

The courage God gave me to make some very crucial decisions spread into other areas of my life. I am no longer afraid to trust my own judgment. I am no longer afraid to be me.

God used cancer to teach us. Cancer taught us to have patience, compassion, humility, and to use wisdom. Now when we pray for someone with a need, we pray believing God can do the miraculous, but we also pray with a better understanding of their struggle with pain and suffering.

If you have lost someone to cancer, or from any sickness or tragedy, knowing it was for a reason doesn't take away your pain. I am so sorry for your loss of their presence. But for however long they were here, it was for a purpose.

Job lost everything. After Job prayed for his friends, the Lord restored him to his former prosperity and gave him double all that he had lost. (Job 42:10) Job had seven more sons and three daughters, the same as before.

Everything Job had was doubled, except for his children. He returned only the same amount back to him. Why? Because Job's other children were still alive in the presence of God and Job will see them again. God does everything well.

Cancer affects every member of your family. It brings pain to one and worry and concern to the others. However, it can also bring them closer together.

Our granddaughter, Autumn, had a school assignment to write a free verse poem. We had no idea she had written about her grandfather until after she turned it into her teacher:

Grandpa's Story

He always wears jeans and a shirt
With pens in his shirt pocket
He sits in a recliner, but not at his house,
Eight long hours he waits
Until the chemo has filled his body
Now he sits in a different recliner, sleeping
at home from the chemo's effect
He even hiccups for 10 days, day and night
After 8 long treatments,
the doctor gives him the news
You are now cancer free Noble
He is now able to play with me.

– Autumn Clay

None of us want to travel the road of cancer. I certainly never thought it would have come to our house, especially through my husband, the rough, tough lumberjack. But nothing comes to us without first passing through God's approval.

In our journey though cancer, I came to the realization that one of the greatest hindrances to our ministry has been the person writing this book. I was the one who felt like we could never measure up. I felt that we were too inexperienced, too unqualified, and certainly not well-dressed enough. My husband never felt any of those things. It was just me.

During his battle with cancer, as I watched him witness to every person he came in contact with about God's love, I had an epiphany:

Ministry is not about me. It is not about us. It's about the people we help. That revelation cleansed all anxiety out of my mind. No more, "What will they think?" or "Are we saying the right things?"

Looking back, I didn't realize how selfish I was. To compare is to separate. No one is inadequate with God. There's nothing to prove. There is just a lot of work to do. There are enough hungry people in the world for all of us to feed.

As I began to grow in this revelation, I stopped feeling incompetent because of our past failures. I stopped feeling like we had to earn the right to do what God had called him to do. Instead, I joined with him.

God has since opened up doors that would not have been possible, because before, I was too afraid to walk through them.

We will all face storms or have trauma in our life. We lose someone close to us, get divorced, lose our job or someone hurts us badly.

More often than not, in some way or another, we come out stronger, wiser and a better person. It is not the survival that makes you stronger, it is the work that you put in as a result of it that makes you better.

When a storm comes into your life, you will wonder how you are going to make it through it. You may even wonder if it is over yet. But one thing is for sure. You will never be the same again. And that is what the perfect storm is all about.

MIRROR NOTE:

Not all storms come to disrupt your life.
Some storms clear your path.

THE END . . .
OR A NEW BEGINNING

The hard times we go through are not intended to hurt us. They are to shape our character into the person God wants us to be and receive his blessings and calling on our life. All you can change is yourself, and sometimes that changes everything. Understand that life is like a book, some chapters must end, but turn the page and continue forward.

All of the lessons from my mirror have helped me grow into the person I am today.

The three greatest lessons I have learned are:

1. *Let go of the past without regret.*

2. *Do not put my hands to things not meant for me.*

3. *Trust God in the process.*

Sometimes, it takes a failure to cause us to look inside of ourselves and find a whole different person that we never knew existed. Age is irrelevant. We can't go back to the past, we can only take the lessons that we have learned and move forward.

Wherever you are in your journey is a starting point.

It can begin with one Post-It® Note.

Change begins with me.

MIRROR NOTES

Failure is a bruise, not a tattoo. – Jon Sinclair

Broken crayons still color. – Shelly Hitz

What happened in your past is not as important as what will happen in your future. – Joel Osteen

Your greatest life message and your most effective ministry will come out of your deepest hurts. – Rick Warren

Sometimes when things are falling apart, they may actually be falling into place. - Unknown

The darkest nights produce the brightest stars. - Unknown

If it doesn't open, it's not your door. - Unknown

I am not what happened to me. I am what I choose to become. – C. G. Jung

Don't compare your life to others, you have no idea what their journey is all about. – Regina Brett

A diamond is a chunk of coal that did well under pressure. – Henry Kissinger

We are in charge of our attitudes – Charles Swindoll

Failure is the opportunity to begin again more intelligently. – Henry Ford

Everything you have gone through is preparing you for what you are called to do.

Don't look back, you're not going that way. – Mary Engelbreit

Every flower must grow through dirt. – Laurie Jean Sennot

Don't give up. Normally it is the last key on the ring which opens the door. – Paulo Coelho

If it's not your story to tell, don't tell it. – Iyanla Vanzant

You may have to fight a battle more than once to win it. – Margaret Thatcher

Everything is going to be ok in the end. If it's not ok, it's not the end. – Oscar Wilde

If I invest in God's dream, God will invest in mine. – Paula Fuller Enloe

FROM THE AUTHOR

This is not the kind of story most of us want to tell. Lessons from my mirror began with something inside of me, pushing me to share them. The process demanded more reflection and soul searching than I've ever done. If I could sum up everything for you that I have learned from this, it would be that you are not alone. Many of us leave our stories untold or our songs unsung. We are tormented by the idea that no one could have made all the terrible mistakes I have. Yet, telling your story may be the most powerful medicine on earth. You become the hero in a novel no one else can write. It does not have to be in words on a book, but the lessons from your own mistakes may be the very ones that help someone else embrace and overcome their own fears.

Thank you for purchasing and reading the lessons from my mirror. Blessings and love to you all. – *Paula*

Connect on Facebook

and Instagram
@mymirrorlessons

CPSIA information can be obtained
at www.ICGtesting.com
Printed in the USA
LVHW080529140220
646904LV00006B/6

9 781728 923550